The Joy of Ageing

This book is a treasure, to be read again and again. The reality of ageing shines through many of the chapters. Not the 'let it go' of the children's *Frozen* film, but the courageous and spirit-filled 'let it be'. We learn to take our hands off directing our lives, inspired by Mary of Galilee's 'Let it be done in me'.

The author reminds us that the ageing process touches us from birth – the 'getting bigger' of children, the 'growing up' of teenage years, and the maturing that goes on until we reach the sixties when the word 'ageing' is spoken to us – usually in a doctor or dentist's clinic!

Brian discusses the phrase 'the grace of dependence'. Though we naturally want to be independent, we are challenged with 'a new thing' being done in us. When we see things clearly and differently, healing can begin. The human heart can hold a capacity to rejoice and a capacity to mourn – perhaps this is the birthplace of our growing in wisdom. As well, Brian confronts society's emphasis on doing and being busy. 'Doing' and 'being busy' are not virtues! Productivity can be replaced by fruitfulness – in relationships, in being, and in our spirituality. To offer or to receive a listening heart is a true gift.

The reality of death's visit is never far from us. Society has set up a fear of dying alone, but Brian reminds us that that is exactly what we all will do. Whether we are fortunate or not to have someone holding our hand, we do die alone – many of us believe, we die into the loving arms of God. This is our call, in faith – a lived faith – 'what I give my heart to' – rather than a list of doctrines.

The sections on prayer are echoes from Brian's own life and his many years of listening to the desires in the lives of the many people who have sought his guidance. He draws us to a contemplative way of living – open to all God's gifts in creation, our own memories and our dreams. I love this one liner: 'Don't try too hard to pray'. Wow! Doesn't that defy the multitude of books we have read and the speakers we have heard with a list of do's and don'ts on the subject of prayer. Thank you, Brian, for sharing your spirit and your prayer with us.

MARLENE MCGRATH, Spiritual Director,
Heart of Life Centre for Spiritual and Pastoral Formation.

At 92 years of age, I am not too bright at summarising, but I can say that this book was a delight to read. I love the positive title and I found that every chapter rang bells for me. I encourage other oldies to read and ponder these reflections: *The Joy of Ageing.*

JOAN MANSFIELD,
Missionary Sister of St John of God, Broome, WA.

This is a wonderful little book, a real gem. *The Joy of Ageing* tells the story of Brian Gallagher's life. When I first read the book, I felt as though the author knew me. I was reminded of the story in John's Gospel when the two future disciples asked Jesus: Where do you live? Jesus' only reply was: Come and see. They spent the rest of the day with him. That is precisely what it was like for me when reading this book.

Brian's chapter on prayer particularly resonated with me. Over the years, I too have set aside a time of prayer every day. A significant time to be with God every day is important to my physical and spiritual health. The prayer of St John of the Cross that Brian quotes summarises what I would want to say about prayer.

There is one other special feature that I found helpful. From his reading of other spiritual writers, Brian has a special knack of citing a sentence or a paragraph to crystalise what he is describing and to affirm his own experience.

All in all, *The Joy of Ageing* reveals the author's own deep spirituality. At the same time, it shows that our personal story has a universality, touching others.

NOEL MANSFIELD MSC,
author of *Dawn to Dusk: Towards a Spirituality of Ageing.*

According to estimates by the United Nations, there are today, worldwide, about 600 million persons aged 60 and over. The total will double by 2025 and could reach two billion by 2050. Based on these figures, Brian Gallagher's book *The Joy of Ageing* will be a best seller for many years to come.

In this book, Brian refers to passages from the Bible, from other religious writers and from books of his own to develop a spirituality for 'oldies' that is personal and relevant to us all, as we age. He writes from his own experience – experience built on support from a blessed family, his own religious life, and long years of ministry as a priest. As an example, he refers to the dream of Martin Luther King to make the point that his dream and our own dreams are to be shared and passed on. Wisdom is passed on in the silence of dreams, the language of God.

While reading *The Joy of Ageing*, I thought of the prophet Simeon. Simeon had waited and waited for the Lord. When he held the child Jesus in the temple, he gave thanks to God. Brian, too, in the twilight of his years, gives thanks to God for his life and his gift of communicating words of wisdom to his readers. I am happy to recommend this book, especially to the older generation.

MICHAEL SIMS MSC,
Chaplain, St Joseph's Home for the Aged, Northcote, Vic.

*Other Books of Brian Gallagher
published by Coventry Press*

Communal Wisdom
Set Me Free
The Eyes of God
God's Foolishness
No Greater Love

BRIAN GALLAGHER MSC

The Joy of Ageing

A SPIRITUALITY FOR OLDIES

COVENTRY
PRESS

Published in Australia by
Coventry Press
33 Scoresby Road
Bayswater VIC 3153

ISBN 9781922589071

Scripture quotations are from the *New Revised Standard Version Bible*, copyright 1989, Division of Christian Education of the National Council of the Churches of Christ in the United States of America. Used by permission. All rights reserved.

Catalogue-in-Publication entry is available from the National Library of Australia http://catalogue.nla.gov.au

Cover design by Ian James – www.jgd.com.au
Text design by Coventry Press
Set in Fontin 11pt

Printed in Australia

Table of Contents

Foreword

Brian Gallagher's *The Joy of Ageing: A Spirituality for Oldies* is a welcome contribution to the growing literature on the experience of human ageing. Two words in the title indicate the author's focus – 'joy' and 'spirituality'. The invitation to enter into a reflective (and slow!) reading, exploring one's experience of growing old is presented in a personally engaging and down-to-earth way. The tempered nature of joy and the grace of ageing provide a springboard for a series of moving meditations on facets of the ageing experience. Brian emphasises the 'tempered' nature of the joy he considers 'a joy not without sorrow, but joy nonetheless' (p. 8). Complementing this focus is his appreciation of spirituality as 'about trust, gratitude, praise of God and compassion for all God's people' (p. 9). These two insights pervade all seven reflections that follow.

As the reader mulls over the sections of this book, there is a sense that the author has presented understandings of ageing and wisdom distilled through the decades of his own faith journey and his ministry as a priest and spiritual guide. He is alert to the diminishment that comes with the years that opens us to the grace of dependence, that poverty of spirit so necessary for a rich inner life. The wisdom 'to be' during one's later years is enriched by the memories of a lifetime. I was struck by his idea that memories show us God's back as he has walked past at different stages in one's life.

Three final meditations suitably round off the author's reflections in *The Joy of Ageing*. Alert to the network of relationships that have peopled our lives, there is much to be grateful for. Living mindfully prepares the ageing person for the self-giving asked of them at death and, before that final act, enriches the task of being present to God in the activity of daily prayer.

This book merits repeated reading. As the author suggests, such reading should be slow and reflective. To do so is to absorb a contemplative approach to the depths present in the unique journey we call ageing – with a tempered joy and a profound sense of God with us!

Laurence J. McNamara C.M.
Navigating Ageing Project
Catholic Theological College, Melbourne

Introduction

My mother was my present age when she said to my sister one day, 'You tell me when I go funny like those old ladies over there'. Ann's response was 'Mum, you're already funny!' I can well understand that: other people were always the 'oldies', weren't they? But there comes a time...

In fact, that time seems to have come quickly, once I started noticing the messages other people were giving me. The lady in the train stood up to offer me her seat, the young fellow across the road came over and took my rake: 'I'll do that for you!' and my doctor kept reminding me that I am now vulnerable (maybe the doc's word for 'funny'?). In fact, I gave the most convincing message to myself in my unexpected enthusiasm for the party celebration of my eightieth birthday a few years ago. I noticed then and since that I am more than happy to be my age. I am quite ready, even 'proud' (humbly proud), to respond to people's 'how old are you?' question. I rejoice to be in my eighties. I am looking forward to my nineties.

Looking forward, looking ahead, seems to be inherent to older age, too: though I can look back on many memories – which I talk about later – I also find that I often look ahead. It reminds me of the child's joy in expectation: *I'm almost four* or *I'll be seven next year*. Remembering 'unless you become as little children...' (Matthew 18:4), I ponder what the child and the child in the old person have in common. Could it be joy?

There is a sense in which both know joy. For the child, it is an excited joy, the joy of playfulness and new discoveries. For the old man or woman, it is more a subdued joy, a joy tempered by life's ups and downs, perhaps the joy of a new perspective on life. Yes, something to look forward to.

I would not want to overlook the 'ups and downs'. I know well that old age is not entirely a happy time for many people, as they struggle with the inevitable disabilities, often the sicknesses, and the need to be cared for. In years past, growing old emphasised the need to avoid sickness and disability. I believe, rather, that acceptance and adapting to the setbacks of ageing is more likely to bring satisfaction. Our attitude to our ageing – how we choose to accept the setbacks and disappointments – is critical. For this reason, in the very first chapter, I emphasise the *tempered* nature of the joy that I speak of, a joy not without sorrow, but joy nonetheless.

Though I try to live in the present moment, I find joy in my memories of what has happened in my life and in my dreaming of what perhaps could yet happen. Gradually, I begin to see my life differently. I see this tempered joy as the grace of ageing. I have experienced it in my own life and I have witnessed it in my close family: my mother died in her eighties, my father lived to 95 and his sister Maggie to 97. Their parents died in their eighties, but their grandmother lived till her one hundredth year. Even in my mid-eighties, I have had some experience of ageing!

I bring that experience to my writing. I write personally, often in the first person. I know that there are theories about ageing, based on extensive research and interviews with older people. I have read books of that nature and will refer to one in particular, but I emphasise that this is my reflection on my own experience – my experience of my own ageing and my experience in observing and listening to my peers. The reader's experience may be different. I would be happy to hear it. Reflective writing invites reflective reading: I suggest a slow reading, maybe one chapter at a time.

Moreover, I'm interested in what a Christian spirituality has to say to our experience of ageing. I reflect on my experience from a faith perspective. Not faith as belief in dogmas, but faith as belief in a loving God, inviting me to trust God's presence and care for me, faith learned from experience. For me, spirituality is about trust, gratitude, praise of God and compassion for all God's people. In the approach I have taken, then, I reflect on the experience of ageing in a prayerful way, what I call a contemplative way, listening always for God's invitation. The chapter on prayer describes this approach and suggests ways of prayer that seem appropriate for older people.

Pope Francis and I are the same age. The Pope often identifies himself with older people. I shall enlist the Pope's support.

Ageing

These days, the term 'ageing' is usually reserved for older age, perhaps over seventy years old. But, in truth, the ageing process begins on day one: we age from the very beginning of our life, hour by hour, day by day, birthday by birthday.

In our early years, we don't call it 'ageing'. Rather, we 'grow up' or we 'mature'. And we delight in doing so: for example, the joy of a child's first unaided walk or a teenager's learning to drive a car or starting their first job are happy times of celebration for most families. There is joy in ageing. We notice, though, that as we continue to age or mature, our joy changes shape. Maybe our joy matures, too. The joy we experience in mid-life, for example after some major decision that turned out well, is a deeper kind of joy. Though quite different from the child's excited joy, we still celebrate – I suspect, in a quieter way, more contented within. This changing nature of our joy is ongoing as we continue to age. In what follows, I discuss the joy of old age.

In older age, as I notice my greying hair and my wrinkling skin, the terminology of ageing makes good sense. More significantly, almost every day, I notice also some experience of diminishment or limitation. It seems I cannot do all I used to do: my previous physical and mental abilities do not seem to work in the same way any longer. Sometimes, I even depend on others to accomplish ordinary tasks.

Understandably, we often struggle to accept this diminishment, this experience of loss. But I know, too, that as we come to terms with such experiences in older age – experiences that are seen as liabilities in mid-years – we can find new meaning in life. I dare to say they may even enrich our life. Kathleen Dowling Singh sees the value of our 'growing list of diminishments' in helping us to wake from the 'dream of self' and open us to new grace.[1]

It is quite unrealistic to imagine that our diminishment is going to improve – as though the ageing process can be reversed! And so, I take for granted that we have accepted and not tried to ignore the aches and pains and the limitations of our ageing. I can suggest two possible ways to live with the limitations, even to know the new life that they offer. Both of these ways are real for me – I hope, not only for me.

First, I remind myself that I cannot expect to be any different from all the other old people I know, some indeed who are finding their ageing much more painful than I am. I align myself with my brothers and sisters: this is our shared experience. If I focus more on other people's struggles, I think I grow in compassion for others and I find that I am less concerned about my own aches and pains. That is certainly new grace, enriching my life.

---

[1] Kathleen Dowling Singh, *The Grace in Aging: Awaken as You Grow Older* (Somerville, MA: Wisdom Publications, 2014), 65.

My second suggestion takes a different approach. I have often heard it said that in this time of diminishment, we need to 'let go'. I know that is true: we do need to let go of some of our past ways and achievements. But these days, I prefer to speak rather of 'letting be', inspired by Mary's 'let it be done to me' in response to the angel's news that she was to be the mother of Jesus. (Luke 1:38). Mary's 'let it be done' seems to me to be her parallel experience to Jesus' entrusting himself to God: 'Father, into your hands, I commend my spirit' on the cross. (Luke 23:46). Both are offering their 'surrender' to God. Let it happen, let God do whatever God wants. Such handing over to God asks deep faith and trust in God. Jesus handed himself over to the same God whom he thought had abandoned him. Mary handed herself over, even though she could not understand how she could be pregnant or what being the mother of Jesus would mean in her life.

For ourselves, noticing and accepting our limitations as we age may well be our experience to parallel Jesus' 'into your hands' and Mary's 'let it be done'. As we say 'ok, let it be', perhaps with some grieving, we are entrusting ourselves to God, allowing God to lead us in our lives. As I have said, this is not easy. Our more spontaneous inclination is the very opposite – most of us tend, rather, to resist handing ourselves over to another's care. To say 'let it be done' is to surrender, to entrust ourselves to God's care.

Cardinal Newman's *Lead Kindly Light* captures this trust:

> *Lead Kindly Light, come lead me on.*
> *The night is dark and I am far from home,*
> *lead Thou me on...*

The second verse acknowledges that he wasn't always so trusting, but the third verse celebrates that there is every reason to be so:

So long Thy power hath blessed me.
Sure it still will lead me on…

Such trusting, handing ourselves over to God, in fact, was Jesus' invitation – and promise:

Very truly, I tell you, when you were younger, you used to fasten your own belt and go wherever you wished. But when you grow old, you will stretch out your hands and someone else will fasten a belt around you and take you where you do not wish to go. (John 21:18)

The Social Justice Statement of the Australian Bishops Conference calls this 'the grace of dependence'.[2]

Grace, yes, but a grace not without its demands: it can be painful, it is quite a struggle for some people. When we are invited to such dependence in old age, it calls on some humility. We are being asked to accept the fact that we are no different from anyone else, we are quite ordinary. Wilkie and Noreen Au use the biblical term 'poor in spirit' to describe this experience of the grace of dependence.[3] Jesus promised abundant blessings to the poor in spirit.

---

[2] ACBC Social Justice Statement 2016-17 *A Place at the Table: Social Justice in an Ageing Society*, 17.
[3] Wilkie Au and Noreen Cannon Au, *Aging with Wisdom and Grace* (New York: Paulist Press, 2019), 43.

> Only once in my life, years ago, I was carried on a stretcher by ambulance officers, carried quite high, if my memory is accurate. I cannot imagine any greater challenge to my self–sufficiency (the 'I can do it' syndrome). Totally at the mercy of others, I had no control, no props, no security – except to trust: the grace of dependence.

Another example of diminishment as we age is that, gradually, we become less concerned about the outer descriptions of who I am – my work, my achievements, my good name – and more content to be me. Just me, 'the name I call myself', as Julie Andrews sang. Gradually, we recognise that these external descriptions of the person I am – that once seemed important to us – in fact, do not define us. We can live without them. Our different perspective knows that there is a much deeper truth to 'me'. I read recently that the coach of a top tennis player cautioned reporters who were extolling the young woman. He told them that 'playing tennis is what she does; it is not who she is!'

When we are young, we tend to engage almost exclusively with the external world. But when we experience the diminishment of older age, we realise that we need inner resources as much as external helps. We discover our inner life. Parker J. Palmer, a highly regarded Quaker author, writes of our 'inner life':

I mean a largely silent, solitary process that helps us reclaim the 'ground of our being' and root ourselves in something larger and truer than our own egos.[4]

Palmer is speaking of what I am calling my 'true self', the deeper truth of 'who I am', the bare me. Too often, we hear the conversation stopper: 'I'm sorry, but that's me, that's who I am!' In truth, that is not who the person is, but rather an unconsciously fabricated self, not one's true self. The conversation stops because the person is unaware of this, even closed to the possibility of any change in themselves.

One's true self, free of those familiar, external trappings and all my imaginings about my reputation and my self-image is not discovered entirely by introspection or self-examination. Only God sees the heart (1 Samuel 16:7). Rather, as I reflect on my varied life experiences, my meetings with other people, my reactions to unexpected incidents, and my memories and my hopes, in some sense God reveals my true self to me. Even in such reflection, I pray that I will see myself truly.[5] Who I am before God becomes clear to me, as I grow in self-awareness and self-knowledge.

When we are in touch with our true self, an offshoot is that we are more able to let other people be their true selves, too – not the self I would like them to be. Again, we become more compassionate towards others, more able to accept others, however different from us.

---

[4] Parker J. Palmer, *On the Brink of Everything* (Oakland, CA: Berrett-Koehler Publications, 2018), 146.

[5] I developed this point in *The Eyes of God* (Bayswater, Vic: Coventry Press, 2019).

On several occasions, I have noticed an older person sitting by herself at a social gathering, it seems quietly and contentedly, maybe even with a half-smile on her face. She doesn't appear to speak very often, but I suspect she doesn't miss what is happening all around her. Indeed, she seems to appreciate the people she watches, witnessed by the occasional gesture towards others.

This woman seems to be quite centred, in her own place, her own space, happy to be herself – what some people term her 'individuality' – though she is not separate from others. I believe that older people like this are in touch with their true self. Which seems to me the reason they can sit quietly and contentedly. I think older people like this know the joy of older age, a very different joy from the joy of earlier life. This is how I understand joy.

In his celebrated play *Murder in the Cathedral*, T. S. Eliot has the Archbishop of Canterbury, Thomas Becket, preaching in his cathedral on Christmas morning in the year 1170.[6] Reflecting on the Mass of Christmas day, the Archbishop notes that it is a celebration of both the birth of Our Lord and his passion and death on the cross – 'at the same time':

> Whenever Mass is said, we celebrate the passion and death of Our Lord. On this Christmas day, we do this in celebration of his birth... Beloved, as the world sees, this is to behave in a strange fashion. For who in the world will both mourn and rejoice at once and for the same

---

[6] T. S. Eliot, *Murder in the Cathedral* (London: Faber & Faber, 1965).

reason?... It is only in our Christian mysteries that we can rejoice and mourn at once and for the same reason.

As I have discussed at length in other writing,[7] the Archbishop talks of this paradox of joy and sorrow at Christmas time and again in the death of martyrs, the following day being the feast of the first Christian martyr, St Stephen:

> We do not think of a martyr simply as a good Christian who has been killed because he is a Christian: for that would be solely to mourn. We do not think of him simply as a good Christian who has been elevated to the company of the saints: for that would be simply to rejoice.

Mourning alone would be unchristian, rejoicing alone would be inhuman. Rather, we rejoice and we mourn at the same time, and for the same reason. Eliot gives us an essential element of true joy: joy and sorrow coexist. Joy and sorrow belong together: they complement one another. In his book on ageing, Edmund Sherman calls this a 'mutuality of opposites'.[8]

This mutuality of opposites describes our tempered joy – a joy tempered by life's experience, by the ups and downs, the struggles and the hard times, the losses, perhaps the failures. The point is that those experiences in life that deserve what Eliot calls 'mourning' do not take away the deeper joy that is God's gift. The gift is more evident as we age and are able

---

[7] See, for example, *God's Foolishness* (Bayswater, Vic: Coventry Press, 2020).
[8] Edmund Sherman, *Contemplative Aging: A Way of Being in Later Life* (New York: Gordian Knot Books, 2010), 40.

to look back on those earlier experiences from a different standpoint.

> I was privileged to lead the funeral service for a top scientist – though a man little known in public. Alex's lifetime research had been into precipitation, rain and dew and frost. The family knew the sadness of his passing, but wanted to celebrate his rich life. At the conclusion of the service, with big smiles all round, they played that happy old hit song: *Raindrops keep falling on my head.* Joy and sorrow in the one experience.

Archbishop Becket was murdered in his cathedral four days later, leaving his people with these words:

I do not think that I shall ever preach to you again. Because it is possible that in a short time you will have yet another martyr, and that one perhaps not the last. I would have you keep in your hearts these words that I say, and think of them at another time.

Another Archbishop, Oscar Romero of San Salvador, now Saint Oscar, was also murdered while saying Mass in more recent times. Romero's parting words were:

If God accepts the sacrifice of my life, may my death be for the freedom of my people. A bishop will die, but the

Church of God, which is the people, will never perish. I do not believe in death without resurrection. If they kill me, I will rise again in the people of El Salvador.

Romero's conviction that he will rise again in the people of El Salvador is a more dramatic way of saying what I suspect is everyone's experience. I have noticed that when I am invited to let go of something (often for no other reason than that it is taken away from me!), strangely I seem to benefit in other ways. Not unlike the person who loses one sense to find other senses intensified. Can we say that we, too, 'rise again'?

Romero's paradox of death/resurrection is the same as Becket's mourning/rejoicing. Indeed, it is the basic Christian paradox – death and new life. It is the way that Jesus taught and lived, and how he died. Sorrow and joy belong together. Dying and rising belong together. This is the tempered joy deeply rooted in our bones – the joy of knowing our true selves, loved by God. I see this as the joy of old age.

To senior Australians, we ask: what will you bring to the table?... Ageing brings gifts: a centeredness that allows one to rise above the frenetic pace of modern life, a sense of history, ... the wisdom gained from past mistakes or failures, a sense of community... (and) the grace of dependence...[9]

---

[9] ACBC Social Justice Statement 2016-17: *A Place at the Table: Social Justice in an Ageing Society*, 17.

Awakening

'The wisdom of old age' has become something of a cliché, hasn't it? I know a number of people I consider wise. My father was one. I wasn't the only person who saw Dad as a wise old fellow and who readily sought his advice. Dad had wide experience and knowledge – and he knew what he didn't know. I once overheard him saying, 'You don't have to know everything in order to know everything!' Another paradox – and, I suspect, a key aspect of wisdom. Indeed, the ultimate revelation of true wisdom came in paradox:

> Consider your own call, brothers and sisters: not many of you were wise by human standards, not many were powerful, not many were of noble birth. But God chose what is foolish in the world to shame the wise; God chose what is weak in the world to shame the strong. (1 Corinthians 1:26-27)

The Sacred Scriptures tell us that 'God's foolishness is wiser than human wisdom' (1 Corinthians 1:25). When I ponder the question about what makes a person wise, I remember also my father's obvious generosity. I have concluded that there is some essential connection between wisdom and generosity. My parents were extraordinarily generous – with their possessions, their time, their advice and their affection. Dad often said, 'It doesn't hurt to be generous'!

My parents may not have articulated it in as many words, but they seemed to know that their blessings in life were not solely *for themselves*. As a result, especially in later life, they held what was 'theirs' quite lightly; they could just as easily share it with others, even give it away. They had nothing to lose! My parents were sensible and cared for themselves and one another, but they didn't cling to what was theirs. They took generosity for granted.

This is to be free: to be able to hold lightly what we call 'ours', rather than holding tightly lest we lose what is ours. It seems to me that such inner freedom is the link between generosity and wisdom. Inner freedom is a fundamental prerequisite of both generosity and wisdom. And I think it comes with ageing.

From what we read in the Bible, it seems that Solomon knew such detachment or freedom. God invited Solomon to ask for whatever he wanted. God is then said to have given to Solomon 'a wise and discerning mind', in another translation 'a heart wise and shrewd', after praising Solomon for not asking for anything *for himself*. (1 Kings 3:5-12). Which tells us that, though it comes as gift from God, wisdom is not given solely for oneself: wisdom is something to be shared. Like all of God's gifts, wisdom comes as gift of God to be shared – the generosity I observed in my parents.

The Scriptures include several books on Wisdom. The wise one – usually thought to be female (in Greek *Sophia*) – is seen as a 'breath of the power of God'. (Wisdom 7:35). It is the power of God breathing in us that sets us free and makes us wise – a reminder that inner freedom and growth in wisdom are the gift of God's work in us, not our own doing or hard work.

I don't claim any special wisdom, but I do notice as I age how my relationships seem more straightforward and my prayer seems much simpler: perhaps life becomes simpler with ageing. Which seems to me to flow from God's setting us free, freeing us from personal traits that we have become attached to, ingrained habits of behaviour, our blind spots. Kathleen Dowling Singh calls this the process of 'awakening'.[10] My focus on growing in inner freedom, Singh calls 'the laying down of self, the letting go of attachment to self'. In Christian teaching, the terminology is 'dying to self' or 'dying to ego'. Singh acknowledges that this is great challenge because 'selfing is deeply ingrained in all of us'.

Carers in retirement homes tell us that the presence of young children and pets can bring out the best in old people. In different terminology, they may well be talking about awakening or becoming more free. I know this in my own life: I have had canine companions for almost twenty years. When my dog is nearby, I notice that I smile more frequently, I become playful, and at least temporarily, I'm not at all concerned for the 'big issues' of my life, the questions that can preoccupy me at other times. Observers have reported that I seem to be a 'different person' when I'm playing with Scobie on the front lawn, some game that Scobie had invented for us. Could that 'different person' be closer to the real me, my free, true self?

Another example of awakening in older people is that our emotions seem to be much closer to the surface. I identify

---

[10] Singh, *The Grace in Aging: Awaken as You Grow Older*. See, for example, page 46.

easily with 'the tears of an old man', a phrase that I heard recently. That we don't have the same defences that we used to, I see as further growth in inner freedom.

In fact, many of life's experiences can free us. A good example is discovering that what seemed like a time of crisis in life turns out to be a time of growth in maturity. I hear older people talk about a *crisis time* in a close friendship, when the relationship seems to be changing, when the friend or partner doesn't seem to be the person 'I thought she was'. It can be quite a painful time of frustration, of what seems like loss, of helplessness to change what is happening. I believe that this is fairly common experience.

I recall the story of the young man asking to be a disciple of the old guru. The guru said, 'Show me your wounds', to which the fellow replied, 'Oh, I don't have any wounds'. 'What?' said the guru. 'Has there been nothing worth fighting for?' I see our 'wounds' as those times of struggle and loss. 'Fighting', I think, means accepting the painful times and hanging in, still believing.

The truth is that those difficult times are times of grace, times of growth, personally and relationally, times when we are being set free. God's foolishness at its best! Usually, we recognise the grace, the new life referred to above, only after the event. In the chapter on prayer, I note a parallel experience for many in prayer, in our relationship with God. Times of struggle with prayer often turn out to be times of grace.

The grace in the example above – the crisis in a friendship – is that the partners come to know one another more truly, in herself/himself, not as we would like the other to be. And they come to love the other purely for the other's sake. At the same time, I think we come to know God more truly, not as we ourselves have imagined God to be – or wanted God to be. This is to grow in inner freedom.

> Some people grow old young. A friend of mine had a little dog called Henry. Henry always looked like an old man – I called him 'old man'. Henry was quite small – I could pick him up and lift him above my head. But size didn't matter to Henry! When he visited my place with its large grounds and bushland, Henry thought he was a big dog and enjoyed exploring by himself. Some people said he was an ugly dog – he certainly wasn't much to look at. But looks didn't matter to Henry! Henry was his own man, content to be Henry.

Another example of what some older people experience as 'crisis' is when we find that we have too much time on our hands. The busyness of earlier years has passed, the constant demands on our time and involvement are no longer, and we don't know what to do with ourselves.

In journals and other publications, there is much discussion about doing and being. Some see the invitation simply to *be* when we find that we cannot do all that we used to do. They argue that this relieves us of any pressure to be productive in our old age. It's true that our culture has a strong emphasis on productivity, but I fear that the encouragement simply to *be* is too simplistic a response. What does it mean for us to be? Hardly relaxing in our favourite armchair all day? In some sense, we will always be doing something. Wilkie and Noreen Au counter being productive with being fruitful.[11] Fruitfulness includes leisure time, play time, quiet time. I suggest that the attitude we bring to our day is the most significant factor, if we are to be fruitful in whatever we do as we age, whether in the armchair or in the garden.

I like to encourage what I call a 'contemplative' attitude to life, not in any monastic sense, but more in the everyday sense of moving at a slower pace, being more attentive to one's surrounds and one's involvements – listening, noticing, waiting in a more receptive way than we might have in the past. This movement towards more interiority as we age seems to come naturally to some people. It may be more accessible to introverted people, but I'm sure it is possible for all, introverts and extraverts. I discuss later some of the helps to developing such an attitude in life, for the sake of fruitful living.

Time on our hands becomes critical when we find ourselves bored, unneeded, lonely. This doesn't happen for everyone, I acknowledge: some older people rejoice in having more free time, time for hobbies they have always wanted to cultivate and movies they have long wanted to catch up on.

---

[11] Wilkie Au and Noreen Cannon Au, *Aging with Wisdom and Grace* (New York: Paulist Press, 2019), 97.

I am grateful to be in the latter group – I have more than enough to occupy myself. But I know the risk of becoming bored is real and that many do experience it.

I think it would be a mistake to take on anything and everything at random, for the sake of relieving the boredom. My suggestion is, rather, to try just sitting still, acknowledging the boredom or the loneliness – let yourself feel this very new experience. I suspect that this, too, may be an invitation for growth in inner freedom. God is wanting to free us from old dependencies that we didn't even know we had! No fault of ours, but it could well be, for example, that feeling good about ourselves in the past depended on keeping busy and helping others and being appreciated for what we were doing. We are now being set free, free to be our true selves.

This is another example of our inner life. One of the gifts of old age is that we are offered the possibility of becoming less self-centred, more free within our hearts – our true self. This again is the Christian paradox: something is lost, but something is gained. Dying and rising. Some of the research on ageing that I referred to earlier believes that this process of awakening brings deeper life satisfaction for older people.[12] Certainly in that sense, our lives are more fruitful. Ah, the wisdom of old age.

We do not lose heart. Even though our outer nature is wasting away, our inner nature is being renewed day by day.
2 Corinthians 4:16

---

[12] See, for example, Edmund Sherman, *Contemplative Aging: A Way of Being in Later Life* (New York: Gordian Knot Books, 2010), 36.

Remembering

Pope Francis wrote that 'the believer is essentially one who remembers'.[13] Citing the memory of Israel and later the memory of Christian people in Eucharist – 'do this in memory of me' – the Pope teaches that memory keeps past experience alive in the present:

> The apostles never forgot the moment when Jesus touched their hearts: 'it was about four o'clock in the afternoon' (John 1:39). Together with Jesus, this remembrance makes present to us 'a great cloud of witnesses' (Hebrews 12:1), some of whom, as believers, we recall with great joy: 'remember your leaders, those who spoke to you the Word of God. *Evangelii Gaudium #13*

Memory is about keeping past experience alive and ever-present. It seems that, as we age, the invitation is to stay in touch with the memories of how God has blessed us over the years. Memory is not so much about past events, but about living in the present. In doing this, we acknowledge that God's blessing is still with us, still present, even in apparently difficult times. However different life is now, maybe even times of sickness or loss, the same God who seemed more obviously present in the past is, in fact, still with us. God is constant, ever faithful. God's love and God's presence do not change:

---

[13] Francis, *Evangelii Gaudium (The Joy of the Gospel)* #13.

I have loved you with an everlasting love. I have continued my faithfulness to you. (Jeremiah 31:3)

We older people, understandably, do look back on memories. It seems to come naturally as we age. And we have the free time and space to do that. I notice that the looking back is often for mere enjoyment – the 'good old days' – though sometimes I look back also for the sake of understanding some aspect of my life, maybe even understanding myself better. I have discussed this latter experience of looking back in the earlier chapter on Awakening.

There are certainly times when we recognise God's presence to us, for example in the beauty of creation or in the face of a dear one, and feel very blessed. But, just as often, I suspect that we don't recognise God's presence till afterwards. This is why our memories become important. The Bible encourages us to look back on memories. There is a lovely story in the Book of Exodus where Moses says to God, 'Show me your face' to which God replies:

> I will be gracious to whom I will be gracious, and will show mercy on whom I will show mercy. But you cannot see my face, for no one shall see me and live. See, there is a place by me where you shall stand on the rock; and while my glory passes by, I will put you in a cleft of the rock, and I will cover you with my hand until I have passed by. Then I will take away my hand, and you shall see my back... (Exodus 33:19-23)

Almost playfully, God tells Moses that he cannot see God face to face, but he can see God's back. In another translation, 'you will see where I have been'.

That may well be the value of our memories: as memories come back to us, often even without our consciously looking back, we can recognise where God has been and how well we have been looked after, even in those times when we weren't aware of God's care. God says to Moses, 'You will see where I have been'.

I think it makes good sense to look back on each day to see 'where I have been'. I have found it a very worthwhile habit to have cultivated. At the end of each day, I quietly ask God to remind me where God has been for me during the day, maybe especially the times when I have not recognised God's presence or God's invitation.

Sometimes, I find myself quite surprised by a memory: as an example, I once found myself remembering a chance meeting that morning with a stranger who approached me to ask about local coffee shops. In prayer, I ask, 'How come I'm remembering that right now? – Dear God, is there some invitation here that I missed at the time?' Slowly, I came to recognise that in my rushing, I had been less than welcoming to the stranger – which, in turn, prompted a prayer of sorrow, asking forgiveness. This quite simple prayer, perhaps for no more than ten minutes, becomes a dialogue with God as I wait and listen, respond, then listen again. I always end by thanking God for the day. Then I can sleep in peace.

Another surprise for me has been that these days I often find myself remembering my ancestors. I have heard other older people speak of this, too. Memories of times I observed my parents or grandparents going about their daily affairs, sometimes conversations with them or with other relatives, stories that have become family treasures, invariably come back to me 'out of the blue'. Just as often – and unexpectedly – I ponder memories of outstanding priests and brothers, my ancestors in church and my religious congregation, men who have touched my life in some way in the past.

Over the years, I seem to have grown in appreciation and love of these people, even identifying with them to some extent. I suspect they are the people whom the church calls the 'communion of saints' – which only now, I recognise includes all of us. And so, I pray with them: I have these countless sisters and brothers standing before God, as it were, on my behalf.

My brother Kevin phoned me to say that our mother had had a severe stroke and had little time to live. I caught a plane home that evening and was at Mum's bedside the next day. All the family spent time at her bedside, in fact for a few more days. As I sat there one day, speaking to her softly, thanking her for everything, just once Mum opened her eyes and looked lovingly into mine. That precious moment held the memory of all the years of our relationship. I always knew my mother's love for me, her first-born. She affirmed it in that moment. I remember saying then, 'That's enough, Mum, thank you'.

In the same spirit of remembering, it makes good sense to look back on my whole life, as well, to see 'where I have been'. Doubtless, people, events, times and places are all stored away in our memory. As we consciously allow them to come into awareness, again there will be surprises. I find that when I do this in a prayerful way, and do it again and again, different memories come to mind, confirming God's care through my life. God says, 'I have carried you, as one carries a child, all the way that you travelled until you reached this place' (Deuteronomy 1:29).

One encouragement that I have found helpful is to see which memories stand out, or which seem to recur more often in my quiet times. Some people even find that there is one stand-out memory, a memory that not only recurs, but which seems almost to define what their whole life has been about. A friend told me of the time, some years earlier, when the first reading of the Sunday liturgy 'swept her off her feet'. Though she had heard the same reading many times, on this occasion God's words in Isaiah 'I have called you by name; you are mine' seemed to be spoken *to her*. She even 'heard' God's name for her, so intimate and personal that she couldn't bring herself to tell me the name. Ever since, God calls her by that name. It is as though the experience of years ago is still happening: the memory is alive and present, God is alive and present. Such memories capture a person's unique relationship with God, who God and I are together.

Pope Francis' conviction that memory brings past experiences into the present, as though I am living those (past) gifts still, reminds us that God will continue to care for us. Our hope for the future is based on our present awareness of how God has cared for us and is caring for us still.

Having spoken of our obviously blessed memories that are still present to us, I know that there are other memories we need to consider. Most of us also have memories that are not so consoling, even painful memories. In my experience, the more unhappy memories are equally present and significant in my life. Maybe my more painful memories and my happy memories can stand side by side.

When painful memories surface for us, memories that we would rather forget – our past sicknesses, our mistakes and regrets, the losses that are part of any life – it seems important to me that we look at these experiences head on, not ignore them or try to forget them. Ironically, when we do try to ignore a memory, it seems to take on more prominence and can affect our healthy living. We learn from experience that we cannot simply forget past memories. But there is a delicate balance between not forgetting and yet not living in the past. There are some memories that we will never completely forget – it may even be important that we do not forget – but in another sense we are invited to leave them behind, lest they rule our lives. In that sense, we do 'forget' these memories.

Healing of memories becomes possible once we are able to be upfront and to name the past hurts and painful times. A first step for many is to talk to some trusted companion about what some past incident was like for me, how it affected me then and still. We do not necessarily have to talk with a professional counsellor. More importantly, we share with someone we trust. And when we know the experience of being heard and understood, accepted, not judged, we begin to see the past differently. That, in itself, is healing.

For this reason, the prayer for healing of memories is recommended. A simple way to pray this prayer is to re-live each painful memory in the presence of Jesus. I know people who spend some quiet time, asking Jesus to accompany them in the re-living of their memory. They talk it over with Jesus. Listening to Jesus' perspective on our memories also helps us to see our experience differently.

Once we begin to see some past experience differently, it takes away the hold that the memory had on us. This is not to deny what has happened for us and how it affected us in the past, but it does lead to a new acceptance. For example, I don't deny or avoid the fact that I was hurt by someone's attitude to me, but I know the experience of forgiving that person, once I see that past time with different eyes – perhaps with some appreciation of the struggles the other person was experiencing.

I know from experience that forgiveness can be resisted, too. To forgive someone who has hurt me, perhaps even without any acknowledgment or gratitude from the other person, can seem like the other is getting off too lightly! But I know, too, that the invitation to forgive past hurts and misunderstandings tends to rise up more and more as we age. Maybe it is another example of our openness to the essential things in life. We may need to ask for the grace to forgive. Jesus had to do that: 'Father, forgive them – for they know not what they do'. Jesus knew that our forgiving another is to share in God's forgiving. Forgiveness, then, frees us from grudges and resentments. Forgiveness brings new freedom, a lightness of spirit.

In a similar way, old age can unearth some regrets around my earlier life: opportunities missed, mistakes made, or times that I have hurt someone else. Again, not to deny that these things happened, it is possible to see them differently from my new perspective on life. The grace of asking forgiveness of another, and of self-forgiveness, comes as I look back and recognise something that I was quite unaware of earlier – maybe the pressure I was working under at that time, or my too-little knowledge of the other person's background. Self-forgiveness also brings new freedom and lightness of spirit.

Healing is all about seeing the past differently, seeing our past from a new perspective, seeing with new eyes. Healing, too, leads to the tempered joy of old age. I may be sad that some event happened in my life, but with healing, seeing the past differently, 'you will see where I have been' and rejoice in that.

Let the memory live again.
(Memories from the musical '*Cats*')

Dreaming

There is an oft-quoted verse in the Bible's book of Joel:

> Your old men shall dream dreams and your young men shall see visions. (Joel 2:28)

Sometimes we hear that dreamers are out of touch with reality. I don't mean dreaming in that sense. Rather, there is a very different sense of dreaming that I imagine the author had in mind: 'Your old men shall dream dreams'. In this chapter, I'm interested in this different sense of dreaming.

I recall the dream of that great civil rights leader in America, Martin Luther King. In 1963, King stood on the steps of the Lincoln Memorial in Washington and addressed the thousands of African-American people who had marched from all parts of the country in the cause of their freedom.

Martin Luther King's speech has gone down in history not only as fine oratory, but as a turning point, a revolution in the American story. It was called *I have a dream*.

> *I say to you today, my friends, so even though we face the difficulties of today and tomorrow, I still have a dream. It is a dream deeply rooted in the American dream.*
> *I have a dream that one day this nation will rise up and live out the true meaning of its creed: 'We hold these truths to be self-evident – that all men are created equal'.*
> *I have a dream that one day on the red hills of Georgia, the sons of former slaves and the sons of former slave owners will be able to sit down together at a table of brotherhood.*

I have a dream that one day even the state of Mississippi, a state sweltering with the heat of injustice, swelling with the heat of oppression, will be transformed into an oasis of freedom and justice.

I have a dream that my four little children will one day live in a nation where they will not be judged by the colour of their skin, but by the content of their character.

I have a dream today.

I have a dream that one day every valley shall be exalted, every hill and mountain shall be made low, the rough places will be made plain and the crooked places will be made straight, and the glory of the Lord shall be revealed, and all flesh shall see it together.

As I developed in my book God's Foolishness,[14] Martin Luther King's dream held both challenge and hope for his people. At the same time, I believe that he was speaking to all of us – and his dream is still relevant. Indeed, the dreams of many oppressed people in our world today are well publicised. King's dream is a perfect example of what I mean by older people looking ahead, as much as looking back on memories. I think there is immense value in our dreams. Martin Luther King's dream helps me to reflect on that.

The first lesson I take from King's dream is that our dreams are to be shared and passed on – they are not solely for ourselves. Indeed, I believe that our dreams are given to us for the sake of all God's people. The same Martin Luther King once said that 'the Church is the place you go out from'. King seems to be suggesting, in my words, that our religious

---

14 Brian Gallagher, *God's Foolishness: A Spirituality of Heart* (Bayswater, Vic: Coventry Press, 2020).

practices (in Church or at home) are not solely to develop a personal relationship with God, but are meant to prepare us to move out, to share what we have been given, to relate to other people, perhaps to care for other people. Reminiscent of the teaching of the much loved Carmelite sister, Teresa of Avila, who told her sisters that the whole point of praying is 'good works'.[15] We may pray quietly in our own corner, but ultimately our prayer will overflow into doing good for others.

Like all the blessings in our life, our dreams are to be shared. This seems to me all the more important for us older people – precisely because our dreams as we look ahead flow out of our different perspective on life. In which case, we do well to listen to one another's dreams – we will learn and we will certainly be challenged. Dreams have potential to change people, many people, not only the one who dreams the dream.

I have heard dreams called 'the language of God'. God speaks to us in our dreams and invites us to personal growth and to 'good works' (quoting St Teresa). As I have mentioned in earlier chapters, something of a recurring theme in my writing is my encouragement to a contemplative way of life, inviting us to wait on God's gift or God's invitation. Our dreams do that for us, for our dreams are clearly given to us – we cannot decide in advance how or what we are about to dream. They are gift, God's gift. I think we can say that our dreams are not only 'the language of God', but they are

---

[15] Teresa of Avila, *Interior Castle* in *Collected Works of St Teresa of Avila* edited by Kieran Kavanaugh and Otilio Rodriguez (Washington DC: ICS Publications, 1976), chapter 4.

expressions of God's dream. Our dreams glimpse something of God's desire for our world. All the more reason to listen to the message of our dreams – and to listen to one another's dreams.

This is not true for all dreams, I know. But I have found that I usually know quickly enough which of my dreams are more significant, which ones I really do need to listen to. Sometimes, there are surprises. Sometimes our dreams won't seem to make much sense – we may well need to talk with someone to be helped to hear the dream's message – but wisdom is like that: 'God's foolishness is wiser than human wisdom' (1 Corinthians 1:25). Once again, it can seem foolish to imagine that a dream of mine might hold some wisdom, something of value, for others as much as myself. But that is how God works.

When Pope Francis said that there is a true vocation and mission set aside for older people, I suggest that this could be a key aspect of that mission: 'Your old men – and women – shall dream dreams'. Could the mission of older people be to dream the dreams that challenge other people to 'good works', to care for one another and to take a stand against injustice and oppression in our world? King's reminder that our dreams – expressions of God's dream – are not solely for ourselves leads me to that conclusion.

Mother Teresa's dream was that all people would know that they are personally loved by God. In Calcutta, she was confronted daily by hundreds of neglected, homeless, dying women and men – a massive social problem. On a blessed visit with her, I witnessed her response: I watched as she spent time with one person at a time, in some instances washing and treating wounds, in others spoon-feeding someone who had no hands. It was as though that single person was the only person who mattered in the whole world. Mother Teresa was living her dream.

Older people, we have nothing to lose. We have 'fought the good fight, we have run the race', we have the experience. We are free to speak up. Our vantage point as we look ahead and dream gives us much to offer God's people.

The other learning for me, as I listen to Martin Luther King again, is that our dreams don't die. It seems to me that our dreams are always relevant: as I have said, there are still oppressed people in our world. Moreover, our dreams are somehow universal; they are picked up elsewhere, even in another time. In his popular song *Imagine*, John Lennon sang 'You may say that I'm a dreamer – but I'm not the only one!' Indeed, there are many. Many of us still dream, as King dreamed, of freedom and justice for all people. Which surely is God's dream.

Over fifty years ago, Pope John's decision that the Church needed a Vatican Council came after he noticed an example of the universality of our dreams. The Pope pointed out how people all over the world are dreaming the same dream – in countries that are quite independent of one another and in situations of very different struggles. He named the dream of working people for a fair wage and a share in profits, the demand of oppressed women for equal recognition in society and in church, and the revolution amongst colonised peoples for self-government. The pope believed that these otherwise independent movements – the same human longing in different disguises – were signs of God's work, God's dream for God's people.

I believe that many older people, after long years of experience, are dreaming the same dream in different disguises. The dreams of we older people, expressions of God's dream, bring to the surface our hopes and our prayers on behalf of all humanity.

I am at the end of my life's story. Yet I feel that I am just beginning... to understand what life is all about. I am developing a new kind of productivity that is simply 'being'. I am moving from doing to being.[16]

---

[16] Noel Mansfield, *Dawn to Dusk: Towards a Spirituality of Ageing* (Bayswater, Vic: Coventry Press, 2018).

Living

Though we remember the past and we dream the future, we live only in the present. Our memories were said to bring the past into the present, keeping our memories alive. So, too, our dreams, our hopes for a better future, invite us to a deeper appreciation of our present reality. We cannot live in the past and we cannot live in the future: we live only in the present, the 'now', one day at a time.

My father taught me – without knowing that he was 'teaching' me – that our relationships are the secret to living happily in the present. Dad used to say, 'Who you know in life is more important than what you know'. Who do we know? Who do we relate to? Who do we trust? This chapter is about our relationships, especially in our older age.

In one of his letters, St Paul listed what he recognised as the signs of God's Spirit working in a person's life. He named the now widely accepted signs: love, joy, peace, generosity... (Galatians 5:22). But then, later, he added one more: God's Spirit, alive and active, is *constructive*: God's Spirit builds – builds relationships, builds community (for example, 1 Corinthians 14:12). All of the experiences underpinning Paul's signs are for the common good. As I have written already, God's gifts to us are not given solely for ourselves: they are to be shared, they are lived out in our relationships. When we find ourselves at peace, in harmony with other people, deepening our relationships, we can be confident that we are on good terms with God. On the flip side, God's presence is not found in disharmony, let alone violent or abusive relationships.

We do seem to become more aware of the relationships in our life as we age. In some sense, we become more dependent on our relationships. Even for those of us who live alone, in many cases by necessity, we find that keeping contact with others is crucial to healthy living. Most of us seem to know that in our bones: though I am happy enough living alone, I'm no hermit! When I write the story of my life, other people will feature prominently.

At the same time, there are people living alone who are quite lonely. Maybe after the death of a spouse, they seem to have very few other relationships in their life. Even while hopeful of other contacts, the challenge for these people is to turn loneliness into a more healthy solitude. I speak of this in the next chapter.

For many people, the closest relationship in their life is with their spouse, partner or dear friend of long standing. It was a great joy for me to watch my old parents, years ago, as they strolled hand-in-hand, secure in their love for one another, not needing to speak of their love, but expressing it in such simple affectionate ways. I know that, over their sixty years together, there were tough times, times of struggle (and I wouldn't know half of them!). It wasn't always like it is now. I suspect that my parents would have found it difficult to articulate how their relationship had developed, but they certainly knew the joy of it in their old age. In more recent years, I have witnessed the same affectionate closeness in other couples, my peers, and have rejoiced with them at significant jubilee celebrations.

In his novel *Two Old Men Dying*,[17] Tom Keneally pictures a couple in their eighties walking side-by-side during a visit to Lake Mungo:

> We held hands and rejoiced in each other's company as we had not necessarily done when young, and bemused by each other's closeness, relishing it! When young I had wondered why the aged were capable of such affection... But death is close and touches are precious, and the beloved remains beautiful even to the aged swain. This had been delightful to discover. (p. 123)

These privileged faithful relationships are classic examples of how our relationships take on extra significance in older age.

To return to my earlier question 'who do we relate to?' A favorite passage of mine from the Sacred Scriptures is 'God has no favourites'. It comes in one of St Peter's sermons (Acts 10:34 and 1 Peter 1:17), though I have slightly adapted the translation. I have pondered that line endlessly and preached on it (too) often. First and foremost, it means that we, all of us, are equally loved by God. It's true that some people seem to get a better deal than others, but the truth is that, whatever the appearances, God has no favourites: we are equally loved. I admit that I cannot say the same: personally, I do have favourites. There are some people of whom I am very fond, and there are others that I find difficult and avoid

---

[17] Tom Keneally, *Two Old Men Dying*, (Melbourne, Penguin Books, 2019).

when I can. Peter's ideal challenges me on the 'who do I relate to?' question. It invites me to be more inclusive in my relationships, more accepting of all people, more tolerant of our differences.

As I age, I have been helped to grow in tolerance and compassion of others by reminding myself that a person's behaviour that sometimes can be off-putting has its own explanation, doubtless in their childhood story. The way someone behaves is not necessarily their free choice and does not necessarily tell us the deeper truth of the person. Jesus knew this in his forgiveness of those who were executing him: 'they know not what they do'. This realisation has certainly been a gift of latter years: God has no favourites.

There is further challenge as our society becomes more inter-cultural. I remind myself that, before all else, we are all people – before we are black or brown, yellow or white, believer or non-believer, local or foreigner. For myself, I need that reminder often. It seems almost inherent in us that we notice differences first. Yes, we are different – but we are equally loved by God. The blessing I notice is that, as I do become more accepting of all people, once again my relationships seem richer and my delight in God's creation seems more joyful.

We older people remind our younger friends also that 'before all else, we are all people'. Sadly, we hear too often of older people – perhaps especially those in aged care and those with dementia – who are not given equal dignity and seen as equally loved by God. It seems reasonable to expect that we will be treated with respect and due care in our ageing. The invitation to accept all people, whatever our differences, is offered to us all.

I used to visit an old priest who had been a missionary for over forty years, now retired. He told me how difficult it had been to leave the Aboriginal people with whom he had lived and ministered all those years. So difficult, in fact, that he couldn't bring himself to tell the people that he was retiring. So he arranged for a boat to wait at the pier at two o'clock in the morning. As he walked to the boat carrying his one case, a loud Aboriginal voice pierced the darkness: 'Come back and leave proper'. John reckoned that those people taught him about 'proper good-byes'. Relationships deserve proper good-byes.

Which reminds me of another constant theme in the speeches of Martin Luther King whom I talked of earlier. He often stressed 'the interconnectedness of all people', of all life. Our lives are so interconnected that 'I cannot be who I am meant to be, unless you are who you are meant to be' – and vice versa. In this, King was ahead of his time: today, the interconnectedness of all reality is prominent in much scientific thinking and writing, as much as in spiritual writing. A more contemporary expression of the same truth is that we are one people. We live in solidarity with all other people and with God's creation.

I notice that older people seem more aware of this experience, as well. Much more so than when we were younger, these days we are more likely to be affected by the news of other people's suffering – the poverty, starvation, homelessness, the disasters in our world. When someone else is hurting, in a real sense I am hurting. Even when our earth is hurting through drought or earthquake, I am hurting, too. This compassion for other people and for creation flows from our oneness, our interconnectedness.

Implied in all that I have said is that our relationships invite gratitude. I spoke of gratitude when discussing our memories, looking back to see where God has been in our lives. I acknowledge significant people in my life, I recognise times of struggle in accepting some people, I rejoice in my connectedness with people of other cultures and other faiths, I smile and I thank God for all these good gifts. In the following chapter, living generously and gratefully is named as the best preparation for our dying. Gratitude permeates our lives. Wilkie and Noreen Au devote a chapter of their reflection on ageing to 'being grateful' and emphasise the importance of 'cultivating gratitude', lest we slip into habits of taking God's gifts for granted or being overcome by our more difficult times.[18] Our attitude to life, not our external circumstances, determines how happy and grateful we are.

At this point, I start to think also of my relationship with God. I talk about our prayer in a later chapter, but I preface that my reminding myself that, in fact, my relationship with God underpins all that I have been reflecting on above. All of our relationships mirror our relationship with God. How we

---

[18] Wilkie Au and Noreen Cannon Au, *Aging with Wisdom and Grace* (New York: Paulist Press, 2019), 116-8.

relate to others is how we relate to God. The saints would go so far as to say that our desire to be close to another person, ultimately, is our desire for God. In Augustine's words, 'Our hearts are restless, O God, until they rest in you'.

Make us know the shortness of our life,
that we may gain wisdom of heart.
Psalm 89

Look back on the past with gratitude.
Live the present with passion.
Embrace the future with hope.[19]

The contemplative is not one who takes his/her prayer seriously,
but one who takes God seriously...
one who is famished for truth,
who seeks to live in generous simplicity, in the Spirit.[20]

---

[19] Pope Francis, *Apostolic Letter to all Consecrated People*, 2014.
[20] Thomas Merton, *Spiritual Direction and Meditation* (Collegeville, MN: Liturgical Press, 1960.) 33.

Dying

In our habit of looking ahead and dreaming, inevitably we find ourselves having to face our death. Indeed, we must do so. The sobering truth is that we will die. All we know and treasure in life is impermanent. I read somewhere that ninety-nine percent of the species that ever existed on our planet are now extinct. Nothing lasts forever.

No person lasts forever. I have noticed how often, when re-living a memory of someone I was close to, maybe a relative or friend, I say to myself 'She is dead now, isn't she?' 'He died, didn't he?' The reality that I can still see someone alive and active, but who is no longer with us, is quite a sober reminder of the cycle of life. We come and we go. 'The days of our life are seventy years, or perhaps eighty, if we are strong' (Psalm 90:10).

In our earlier years, death raises its head only when someone else dies. But it is a different experience for us older people, for the 'someone else' who has died frequently enough is close to our age, or may even be an old friend. It could be me! The reminder of our mortality comes to us and will keep coming, without our bidding. We do well to dream of our dying.

I know that many people are fearful of death. Many years ago, Ernest Becker wrote a prize-winning book entitled *The*

Denial of Death, describing accurately the pervasive anxiety in modern cultures surrounding death.[21] I hear this in people's questions: how and when will I die? whatever does after-life mean? what will happen to my body – and to all my precious collections? how will my family manage after I die?

While this chapter acknowledges our understandable fears, my hope is that my reflection will serve to promote the integration of our spiritual values.

One aspect of the inevitability of death is its timing. We know not the day nor the hour! We may well speak of preparing for death, but in another sense, we need to be ever ready. There is/may be no time for preparation. We can prepare a meal for this evening – we know the time we would like to eat. We can prepare for our anniversary next year – we know exactly how many months before that is due. But 'preparing' for our death is quite a different use of the same word.

The other inevitability of death is that we die alone. We will be blessed if loved ones are able to be with us as death draws close. But in the moment of death, we are alone. Alone with God – though there is no promise that we will be aware even of God's presence in the moment. In his book, *Dancing to My Death*, popular Irish priest Daniel O'Leary writes of his personal experience of nearing death. O'Leary speaks starkly of the 'desolation', the 'abyss of endless falling away' and

---

[21] Ernest Becker, *The Denial of Death* (New York: Free Press, 1973).

'one of the lowest points of my life',[22] reminding us that the aloneness at death can be very painful for some people. He recalls how Jesus felt quite abandoned by God when he was close to death. Is it even possible to prepare for such a time?

> Years ago, I visited my Uncle Jack who was in hospital near to death. We chatted easily, finally about dying. I said to him: 'Uncle Jack, are you ready to go to God?' His reply was, 'I've been ready all my life'.

Granted death's inevitability and knowing that we are using the word 'prepare' somewhat differently from everyday use, still we ask how do we prepare for this moment of meeting God – when we have never experienced anything like it before.

I suggest that, as we trust God's constant love for us, God's promise to be with us till the end of time, the best preparation for death is to live every day well, one day at a time. As I live today, I will live tomorrow, and the next day, and the next... and the day of my dying. Indeed, each day may be my last day, which makes each day all the more precious.

Pope Francis has spoken about death, too:

Death must be faced and prepared for as a painful and inescapable passage, yet one charged with immense

---

22 Daniel O'Leary, *Dancing to My Death: With the Love Called Cancer* (Mulgrave, Vic: Garratt Publishing, 2019).

meaning. For it is the ultimate act towards those we leave behind and towards God whom we go forth to meet.[23]

Our dying is our 'ultimate act' towards the dear ones we leave behind and the God we are about to meet. Our death is the ultimate act of self-giving, our final entrusting ourselves to God, believing in God's promise of life. In the words of the Eucharistic prayer, 'in your kingdom, there will be no more sadness, no more tears, no more suffering'. At the same time, we entrust to God all those who have been and are close to us. Maybe that is the sense in which the Holy Father believes that our dying, or how we die, will be a gift to other people.

In different terminology, Singh sees our ultimate act towards those close to us happening in our 'life review' as we approach death:

> We can savour what is to be savoured with gratitude, forgive what needs to be forgiven with wisdom and compassion, examine what needs to be healed, and focus tender attention on those aspects of our psyche that have remained confused and wounded for so long. Then we can let it all go – the wounds, the defences, the stories and the self who told them.[24]

She says that such review near the end of life can bring immense gratitude and love for the people who are close to us. Singh's life review is not unlike my suggestion in an earlier chapter that we look back, even daily, to see where

---

[23] Francis, *Misericordia et Misera (Mercy and Misery)* apostolic letter to conclude the Jubilee Year of Mercy, 20 November 2016.

[24] Kathleen Dowling Singh, *The Grace in Aging: Awaken as You Grow Older* (Somerville, MA: Wisdom Publications, 2014), 231.

God has been for us. I believe that we are living the ultimate act of self-giving every day of our lives, not solely at the time of our death. There are opportunities for self-giving every day, especially in our relationships, in how we care for one another, how we meet and greet even the stranger, how we respond to the unexpected interruptions to our daily routine.

We are preparing for our death every day, even when death is far from our minds. The moment of our final handing over to God will be the next moment in a life lived generously and gratefully.

In which case, the question becomes how can we help ourselves to live generously and gratefully every day. Numerous writers have made suggestions, not all of which are necessarily helpful to everybody. I offer only what has seemed to help me. I'm sure others will add from their experience. Each to their own!

First, when speaking of wisdom in an earlier chapter, I noted the paradox of opposites co-existing. Whenever we speak of growing in wisdom, we keep encountering this paradox: our ability to hold apparent opposites in harmony. More examples have emerged for me in recent times as I have learned the importance of a balanced life-style. For example, I balance keeping active as I age – exercising, gardening, pottering in the shed – with intentional and regular down-times of rest and relaxation. I balance involvement with neighbours and friends, social outings, with space and time for myself, usually sitting quietly with a good book or good music, or sometimes just sitting quietly.

A balanced lifestyle helps me to appreciate life, to be more aware of the gift that each day brings. When I go back to the garden after rest time, I enjoy it all the more. When I go back to my community of friends after separation, I seem to value them all the more – I feel more connected. This is doubtless where the old saying came from: 'absence makes the heart grow fonder'! Sometimes, periods of separation are imposed on couples – maybe work away from home, maybe a need to care for unwell parents. The choice to accept these times of separation makes the reunion all the richer. Indeed, even when it is not imposed on us, there is immense gain in the free choice occasionally to be alone, in solitude.

Henri Nouwen wrote about the movement from loneliness to solitude that I referred to in the previous chapter.[25] Loneliness is painful, a feeling of insufficiency: 'no one loves me'. Whereas solitude is wholeness, not at all lonely – the inner freedom I spoke of above. It seems to me that I will be more ready to accept the aloneness at the moment of death, however painful, if I have known something of the beauty, even the joy, of aloneness already in my life. I know many older people who consciously opt for times of aloneness, relishing their solitude, content to spend time quietly in their inner world.

The second area that has been helpful for me is that I try to live mindfully, one day at a time. As best I can – and I forget often – this means living in the present moment, being fully present to whoever I am with, wherever I am and whatever I am doing. Another word might be 'attention', being fully attentive to the moment, what some call 'the eternal now'. I do forget often: for example, I catch myself when I am

---

[25] Henri Nouwen, *Reaching Out* (London: Collins, 1976), 26-60.

planning ahead, maybe tomorrow's gardening or next week's meeting, while I'm presently watching and listening to a symphony concert.

I notice that, when I am more present to where I am and what I am doing, an offshoot is that I seem to enjoy what I am doing all the more, whether my daily walk around the lake or my quiet reading and writing at home. Moreover, giving my attention more to the present moment saves me from over-concern with whatever the future holds for me – all those 'what if...' questions. Indeed, a deepening appreciation of the gifts of the present time is the ground for any hope in a future. In the following chapter, I mention some of the prayer practices that seem to help this practice of mindfulness.

Finally, I believe that faithfulness to my morning meditation time is crucial. Ironically, I don't really know how it helps – but it has become non-negotiable. I'm aware that not everyone of us necessarily sets aside daily meditation time. I would want to encourage such a habit – and call it what you will: quiet time, sitting still time, alone time. I see it as the time when I am most obviously entrusting myself to God. Sometimes, lovely memories come back and I enjoy them again. Sometimes, questions pop into my awareness, reminding me that God is present and active in my quiet: are there people whom I have not forgiven or haven't yet thanked? Who have I not loved well? What unfinished business am I resisting? I'm sure these questions are inspired – I don't have immediate answers, but I trust that the answers also will be inspired, as I let the questions sit there in my awareness. In that way, I expect that my quiet prayer times bear fruit in my life – and my preparation for death.

These suggestions were in response to my own question about helping ourselves to live generously and gratefully to best prepare for death. I stand by those practical helps – I need such helps – but I know too that God's loving embrace in the moment of my final surrender will not depend on my life-style or my prayer practices. God's gift of Godself is just that: gift.

Interestingly, all of the above expressions of my desire to live generously and gratefully are found in the theory of ageing called *gerotranscendence*. I was fortunate to read Edmund Sherman's book, *Contemplative Aging*, after I had already written the above.[26] On a number of levels, Sherman describes my experience fairly accurately! He cites Lars Tornstam who developed the theory of gerotranscendence after extensive interviewing of older people in Sweden.[27] *Gero* is taken from the Greek word *geron* for an old man or older person, and *transcendence* refers to the natural tendency in older age to transcend or rise above past habits, ways of thinking and looking upon reality.

In different terminology, I have described my own and others' growing freedom from past concern about my image, my reputation, my job, my ego. This is transcendence. Both Tornstam and Sherman claim that their research

---

[26] Edmund Sherman, *Contemplative Aging: A Way of Being in Later Life* (New York: Gordian Knot Books, 2010).

[27] Lars Tornstam, *Gerotranscendence: A Developmental Theory of Positive Aging* (New York: Springer Publishing Company, 2005).

indicates that this movement of transcendence bears fruit in relationships, in 'everyday wisdom', in less need for approval and prestige, in a decrease in self-centeredness and increased desire to understand oneself, and in inner harmony and life satisfaction.[28] I insist that I was not one of their interviewees, but as far as I can judge, my personal experience is consistent with their findings. For example, I noted earlier our awareness of ordinariness as we age: we are no different from anyone else. Before God, we are equal, one with all creation, a oneness that enriches our relationships – with other people, with creation, with the cosmos. This, too, is transcendence, transcending boundaries between ourselves and other people and creation.

Though not the focus of these researchers, I believe that, while our relationships are enriched, our relationship with God also deepens as we grow in inner freedom and transcendence. I talk about that in that chapters that follow.

◇◇◇

Thomas More to beloved daughter Meg, while being led to his execution:

Have patience, Margaret, trouble not thyself. Death comes to us all. Even at our birth, death doth but stand aside a little. And every day he looks towards us and muses somewhat to himself whether that day or the next, he will draw nigh. It is the law of nature – and the will of God. You have long known the secrets of my heart.[29]

---

[28] Tornstam, 150-1.
[29] Robert Bolt, *A Man for all Seasons* (London: Heinemann Educational Books, 1960).

Praying

Pope Francis once said that older people are to be 'poets of prayer'.[30] I must have spent hours reflecting on that. Whatever did the Pope mean by 'poets of prayer'?[31]

Personally, I'm not a poet. I cannot write poetry, and I admit that I don't always appreciate other people's poems. But could writing poetry be like the dreaming that I reflected on earlier? I hear people say that they don't dream, but I know that we all do dream. I'm not a poet, but maybe I could be – well, in my own way. Maybe all of us could be poets in our own way. Our own way!

Once, inspired by a statue of Teresa of Avila called *Teresa in Ecstasy*, I wrote quite spontaneously:

Ecstasy
Wide open mouth
Wide wide opened heart

That is not strictly a poem, I know. Nor is it strictly a prayer. Its only claim to any fame is that the words seemed inspired when I wrote them. It was as if someone else was writing. The words were given to me.

---

[30] Address of Pope Francis on role of grandparents in the family, reported in *L'Osservatore Romano* 11 March 2015.

[31] Sections of this chapter are based on the chapter on prayer in my book *The Eyes of God* (Bayswater, Vic: Coventry Press, 2019)

Another example came one morning as I woke from a dream. I heard myself saying these words:

I will see
the face of God
in her loveliness

The words were given to me. I suspect that that is the way of good poetry and good dreaming: it is inspired. To see prayer, too, as inspiration has helped me in my reflection on prayer in our lives. Prayer is one of the ways – an important way – in which we consciously focus on our relationship with God, on who God is for us. As I have said, at the same time we are acknowledging the importance of all the relationships in our life.

'The Spirit helps us in our weakness, for we do not know how to pray as we ought, but that very Spirit intercedes with sighs too deep for words...' This line from Romans 8:26 suggests that we should 'let the Spirit pray in us'. I like that. Listening to my own and to other people's experience, I recognise that, as we age, we do become more able and willing to let the Spirit pray in us. As I reflected earlier, we seem more ready to let God take over. We find ourselves naturally pondering life's questions and perhaps God's surprising providence in our life. We become more receptive, more open to God and to other people. We don't neglect our own wisdom, but it seems we become freer about it. We seem able to hold our opinions more lightly, without having to insist on our own way. That makes a big difference to the way we pray.

If we are to let the Spirit do the work, to pray in us, then we don't have to work so hard ourselves, we don't have to try hard to pray. We can wait on God's Spirit, God's inspiration. When we are sitting quietly or when we are taking our daily walk, we do just that. We sit, we walk, we are present to where we are and what we are doing – and we wait on God's inspiration. I think that being prayerful is more important than all the 'how to pray' advice. Maybe being prayerful is more important even than saying prayers.

Still, many of us do like to set aside some regular time to listen again to God's presence and God's invitation in our lives. I notice that when I do that, I don't seem to need many words to pray these days. It seems that all I need to do is to slow down (which is happening already in other areas of my life – no surprise in that, I'm sure) and to be present to where I am and what I am doing – which is to be present to God. Occasionally, some new inspiration comes, some new insight or some sudden awareness of God's gift. And sometimes I do unexpectedly burst into words, words that seem to come from nowhere.

We know that the slowing down needs to be in our inner life, not only in the external, more physical activities. We need to slow down our mind and we need to slow down our expectations on what we think should be happening when we pray. I have learned that to focus on my breathing, deep breaths inhaling and exhaling, slows down my active mind. Many uninvited thoughts do still come into my head. But when I am concentrating on my breathing, they come and they go. I am happy to let them go.

And the desire to be present to where I am and what I am doing means putting aside all other planning and thinking about what to do this evening or tomorrow. This can be helped by having just one focus, maybe a word or a phrase, a mantra, or even a visual object. I notice how people who visit my place often sit for ages simply looking at the view. The rhythm of the waves is enough to hold their attention and keep them in the present moment.

If some inspiration from God does come, gratitude flows spontaneously. But if nothing at all comes to us in these times, it serves as a reminder that we are totally dependent on God's gift – we cannot make anything happen ourselves. I know I am not the one in control, so I trust God's Spirit working in me and, with Mary, I say 'let it be done' to me.

> The poems of St John of the Cross have been important for me in recent years. This is John's prayer from a verse in his Spiritual Canticle:[32]
>
> > You looked with love upon me, and deep within, your eyes imprinted grace. This mercy set me free, held in your love's embrace, to lift my eyes adoring to your face.
>
> I wonder how often John prayed that prayer. I pray it almost every day.

---

[32] John of the Cross, *Spiritual Canticle*, stanza 32. This translation is taken from Marjorie Flower, *Centered on Love* (Varroville, NSW: the Carmelite Nuns, 1983, reprinted 2002).

What I am suggesting is usually called a *contemplative* way of praying. I have referred already to a contemplative way of life. The term 'contemplation' simply means being open to God, open to whatever life brings, open to whatever happens when we sit quietly with God.

When we were taught to pray, saying prayers, the emphasis was on what we had to do or say ourselves. For example, in prayer of petition we usually know in advance who or what we want to pray for. Which is fine – there is certainly a place for that prayer, the way we pray with prayer books and in liturgical prayer. Or many of us like to pray by reflecting on the Scripture readings from Mass, often finding application to our lives. This is a beautiful prayer, certainly to be encouraged. But I sense that, as we age, the prayers that we prayed in our earlier years don't have the same attraction that they used to. Our prayer seems to become less wordy, quieter, simpler, more open to God's Spirit praying in us. Such a way of prayer seems to be a normal and common development for most people, as we age: we simply become more prayerful.

I have had the experience myself – and I have met the same in numbers of other people – when setting aside time for prayer seems almost like a waste of time, when I get no satisfaction from it and when I wonder even whether there is any point in praying. More painful is when I find myself doubting God, as though I have been kidding myself all these years. When this happens, I know people who blame themselves, and imagine that they have to try harder or maybe find a better prayer book. I have met other people who simply stop praying – it's not worth the time and effort! This is a critical time for many older people.

61

Some will find this hard to believe, but I have discovered that there is nothing wrong when our prayer offers no consolation in this way. I believe that it is quite normal. In ways, admittedly different from the past and different from our expectations, God is still present and caring. It can be a real challenge to believe that God is present and caring when it feels like God is not! But this may well be a time when we are being set free from unreal images of God and unreal expectations on our relationship with God. We are being led into wholeness.

In his book *Reaching Out*, Henri Nouwen also teaches that another of the key movements of our lives is when God leads us from illusion to true prayer.[33] We are freed of any illusions about God and about our relationship with God, and led into truth. Not unlike the experience I described earlier as we grow in wisdom, this too is a time for renewed trust in God. John of the Cross recommends that we remain 'in rest and quietude... content simply with a loving and peaceful attentiveness to God'.

The God of our joys and our sorrows, the God of our memories, our hopes and our dreams is the same God who promises 'I will never leave you' (Deuteronomy 31:6). Indeed, nothing can separate us from the love of God (Romans 8:38, 39).

Silence is the language of God.[34]

---

[33] Henri Nouwen, *Reaching Out* (London: Collins, 1976), 105-147.

[34] Dag Hammarskjold, *Markings* (London: Faber and Faber, 1964).

A Personal Word

I have been a Catholic priest for over fifty years. I have been a teacher, a preacher, a spiritual guide, a listener, a reconciler. Most of my ministry has been with individuals and small groups. Occasionally. someone thanks me for a timely word or suggestion, perhaps even a sermon, but more often than not, I receive no feedback and have no follow-up. From time to time, I find myself wondering what happened to a certain person, how did they live their life after those few meetings we shared. But, for the most part, I don't know – and I don't try to find out. Nor do I talk to others about such confidential meetings with others. It seems to me that I am being invited to entrust to God all the people to whom I have ministered.

What I am describing of my life is not unique to me, I'm sure. I know it is a not uncommon experience for older people: 'What have I done with my life?' 'There seems little to show.' 'Does my life have any meaning?' The glib answer would be 'does it matter?' After all, 'naked I came from my mother's womb, naked I shall return' (Job 1:21). I agree that it would be some comfort to have answers – a little boost to the ego – but, in truth, does it matter? I recall once when I tried to say something of these questions to friends, the response was almost protesting, assuring me that my life has had immense value and that I have done much good for other people. I hope I was gracious in my response to them, but their affirmation hasn't taken away the questions!

I believe now that we need to live with such unanswered questions about our life. Even after I list all the happy times, all the gifts, all the people I love and who love me, all the people who have asked my guidance – for all of which I am ever grateful – still 'there seems little to show for my life.' Living with that truth, not knowing answers to my life questions, seems to me a healthy aspect of the diminishment – and the joy – of old age.

When I stand before God, maybe all I will need to say is, 'Here I am, Lord'. Then, dear God, 'I shall see you as you are, I shall become like you, and I shall praise you forever'.[35] Amen.

---

[35] Eucharistic prayer 3.

Recommended Reading

Australian Catholic Bishops' Conference. Social Justice statement 2016-17: *A Place at the Table: Social Justice in an Ageing Society.*

Wilkie Au & Noreen Cannon Au. *Aging with Wisdom and Grace.* New York: Paulist Press, 2019.

Brian Gallagher. *The Eyes of God: Living Discernment.* Bayswater, Vic: Coventry Press, 2019.

Noel Mansfield. *From Dawn to Dusk: Towards a Spirituality of Ageing.* Bayswater, Vic: Coventry Press, 2018.

Daniel O'Leary. *Dancing to my Death: With the Love called Cancer.* Mulgrave, Vic: Garratt Publishing, 2019.

Parker J. Palmer. *On the Brink of Everything: Grace, Gravity, and Getting Old.* CA: Berrett-Koehler Publishers. Inc., 2018.

Edmund Sherman. *Contemplative Aging: A Way of Being in Later Life.* New York: Gordian Knot Books, 2010.

Kathleen Dowling Singh. *The Grace in Aging: Awaken as you Grow Older.* Somerville, MA: Wisdom Publications, 2014.